The Little
Philo

GW01182687

Bill Tomkiss
&
Rick Armstrong

Fisher King Publishing
The Studio, Arthington Lane,
Pool-in-Wharfedale,
LS21 1JZ,
England.

The Little Book Of Philosophy

ISBN 978-1-906377-49-6

The Little Book Of
Philosophy

Bill Tomkiss & Rick Armstrong

Dr Bill Tomkiss was a senior lecturer in Philosophy. For many years he taught undergraduate and post graduate students as well as supervising a number of research projects. His own research focused on language and meaning and during his career he wrote on language, meaning, human rationality and the importance of history and culture in the formulation and expression of meaning. He lectured in a variety of places including Durham and Newcastle as well as Leeds. He has also been guest speaker at a number of philosophy conferences.

Rick Armstrong has a background in management consultancy, advertising, training and marketing. For two decades he worked in the Middle East. He was CEO of a law firm specialising in matters of state based interests. He is the founder of Mentor Group. He is an inspirational speaker regularly presenting on topics such as business creation, motivation and leadership skills. He is co-author of The Little Book of Positive Thoughts and The Little Book of Visualisation.

philosophical

words to

inspire

meaning

life

human

inspiration

words to
inspire
you

desire

nature

nurture

you

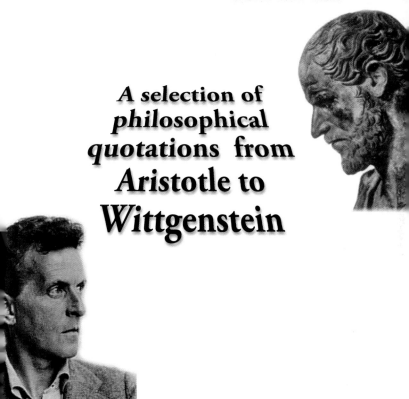

A selection of *philosophical quotations* from **Aristotle to Wittgenstein**

Miracles in the world are many, there is no greater miracle than man.

Socrates

Man is the measure of all things, of those that are that they are, of those that are not that they are not.

Protagoras

The best thing for a man is to pass his life so as to have as much joy and as little trouble as may be.

Democritus

The good and the true
are the same for all
men, but the pleasant
is different for
different people.

Democritus

There is none so worthless whom Love cannot impel, as it were by a divine inspiration towards virtue.

Plato

**All men
by nature
desire to
know.**

Aristotle

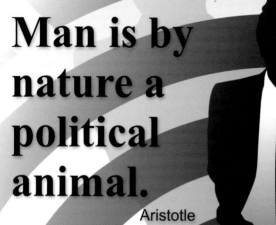

Man is by nature a political animal.

Aristotle

Nature does nothing in vain, nothing superfluous.
Aristotle

We do not wish to know what bravery is but to be brave, nor what justice is but to be just.

Aristotle

Friendship is one of the virtues or at any rate implies virtue. Moreover it is one of the prime necessities of life.

Aristotle

The beautiful is that good which is pleasant because it is good.
Aristotle

Pleasure is the beginning and end of happy living.

Epicurus

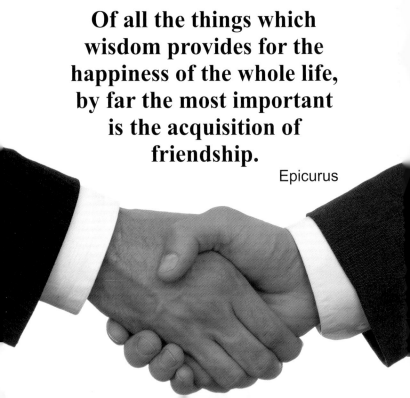

Of all the things which wisdom provides for the happiness of the whole life, by far the most important is the acquisition of friendship.

Epicurus

**Truth comes
out of wine...
In vino
veritias.**
Pliny the Elder

It is when I struggle to be brief that I become obscure.

Horace

For I do not seek to understand in order that I may believe; but I believe, that I may understand.

Anselm

Knowledge and human power come to the same thing.

Francis Bacon

Nature cannot be conquered except by obeying her.

Francis Bacon

I think therefore I am.

Descartes

We are in a special way masters of our actions and thereby merit praise or blame.

(Descartes)

The heart has its reasons which the reason does not understand.

(Pascal)

The human intellect is
liable to err, not only
through the fallibility of
the senses, but also solely
through its own nature.

(Spinoza)

Man is a social animal.

(Spinoza)

Without mutual help men can hardly support life and cultivate the mind.

(Spinoza)

Whatever we imagine is finite. Therefore there is no idea or conception of any thing we call infinite.

(Hobbes)

**Experience
concludes
nothing
universally.**
(Hobbes)

So that in the nature of man we find three principal causes of quarrel. First, competition; secondly, diffidence; thirdly glory.

(Hobbes)

Growing up in a constant attention to outward sensation (men) seldom make any considerable reflection on what passes... till they come to be of riper years; and some scarce ever at all.

(Locke)

We can have knowledge no further than we have ideas.

(Locke)

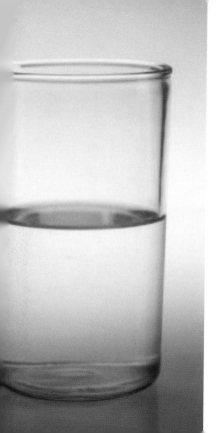

A true sceptic will be diffident of his philosophical doubts as well as of his philosophical conviction.

(Hume)

Custom is the great guide of human life.

(Hume)

The first notion of justice springs not from what we owe to others, but from what is due to us.

(Rousseau)

What I feel to be right is right, what I feel to be wrong is wrong… it is only when we haggle with conscience that we have recourse to the subtleties of argument.

(Rousseau)

conscience

Man is born free and everywhere he is in chains. One thinks himself the master of others and still remains a greater slave than they.
(Rousseau)

The man who needs a lord
is an animal; as soon as he
becomes a human being
he no longer needs a lord.

(Herder)

So act as to treat humanity always… as an end and never merely as a means.

(Kant)

Without man the whole creation would be a mere desert, in vain and without... purpose.
(Kant)

I limit myself in my appropriation of freedom by the fact that I also recognize the freedom of others.

(Fichte)

The purpose which we set for the future conditions our account of the meaning of the past.

(Dilthey)

Is not life a hundred times too short for us to bore ourselves?

(Nietzche)

We are still being constantly
lead astray by words and
concepts into thinking things
are simpler than they are.

(Nietzche)

A high culture can exist only on a broad basis, on a strongly and soundly consolidated mediocrity.

(Neitzche)

Actions are right in proportion as they tend to promote happiness, wrong as they tend to produce the reverse of happiness.

(J.S. Mill)

Happiness is not an abstract idea but a concrete whole.

(J.S. Mill)

The development of individuality is one of the principal ingredients of human happiness, and quite the chief ingredient of human and social progress.
(J.S. Mill)

The great political superstition of the past was the divine right of kings. The great political superstition of the present is the divine right of parliaments.

(Spencer)

Commerce is the natural enemy of the producer.

(Fourier)

Each worker is at war with the mass and bears ill will towards it from personal interest.

(Fourier)

Men who have no touch of genius may have much imagination.

(Schopenhauer)

Truth consists in a conformity of something independent of his thinking it to be so, or of any man's opinion on that subject.
(C.S. Peirce)

Rationalist are the men of principles, empiricists the men of facts.

(William James)

A person is a certain series of experiences.

(Bertrand Russell)

**All human activity
springs from two sources;
impulse and desire.**

(Bertrand Russell)

The lover, the poet and the mystic find a fuller satisfaction than the seeker after power can ever know, since they can rest in the object of their love.

(Bertrand Russell)

Beauty is useful because it is beauty, because a constant need for beauty and its highest ideal rests in mankind.

(Dostoevsky)

However I may twist the speculative answers of philosophy I receive nothing which resembles an answer.

(Leo Tolstoy)

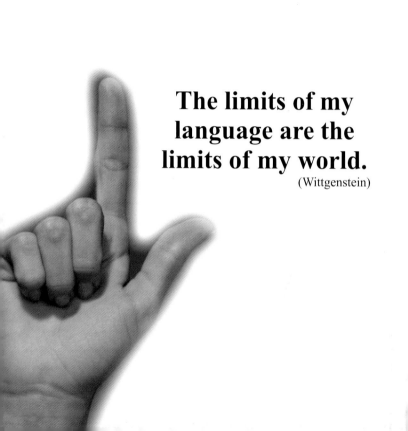

The limits of my language are the limits of my world.
(Wittgenstein)

Philosophy simply puts everything before us. It neither explains nor deduces anything.

(Wittgenstein)

Whereof we cannot speak, thereon we must be silent.

(Wittgenstein)